My Grandma Sings

A Journey Through Dementia to Long-Term Care

Andrea E. Fray

My Grandma Sings
Copyright © 2020 by Andrea E. Fray

All rights reserved. No part of this publication may be reproduced, distributed, or transmitted in any form or by any means, including photocopying, recording, or other electronic or mechanical methods, without the prior written permission of the author, except in the case of brief quotations embodied in critical reviews and certain other non-commercial uses permitted by copyright law.

Tellwell Talent
www.tellwell.ca

ISBN
978-0-2288-2898-3 (Paperback)

This book is dedicated to my children (Naomi & Rihanna) and loving parents (Allan & Eugenia). Your courage and strength in dealing with this illness has been amazing.

Let us continue to raise awareness and advocate for those we love. I would also like to acknowledge my friends who surpassed my expectations that I refer to as my chosen family.

Thank you for helping the girls and I overcome many obstacles during our caregiving journey. Words cannot express my gratitude (Doreen, Dagmar, Dr. Grant, Dr. V, The Campbells, Angela, Trisha, Evon, Michelle, Jameelah, The Johnsons, Cindy, Wayne, Rita, Andrea, Marcais, Melissa, Alma, Dionne, Sharon, Karen, Jacquie, Tony, Hilda, Olivia, Neelam, Alphia, Delta, Joan, Allison, Emereth, Debbie, Maureen, Kevin, Barry, Veronica, Freddie, The Henry's, Simone and Comfort). May God continue to bless and keep us all.

    Love Always,
    Andrea

My Grandma sings on the choir… and has the most elegant attire.

I look forward to spending time with her when my parents are away, holidays, weekends, or on a rainy day.

We like to bake cakes together, go to the movies, and plant flowers. If the weather is nice we go for walks and talk for hours.

As I got older Gran would grow to. She started to forget things. I did not know what to do. She could still prepare food, and knew all the words to our favourite songs.

However, she would forget people. Say silly things like refer to a church as a steeple. She began to mix up names, dates, and times. Repeat the same stories (over a million times) time after time.

Her fashions were questionable, she got out a lot less, refused to be questioned, and the house was a mess.

"It's normal". She's aging" my parents would say. "If you're really worried well go to see the Doctor today. The doctor asked her questions, followed by noting her height, and her weight. Then ordered blood tests and CAT Scans, while we continued to wait.

One week later the results were in "Dementia" they called it meaning her memory was wearing thin. When it comes to processing new information her understanding was grim.

Grandma would need a warm and loving environment that was safe and secure. With doctors and nurses and the odd pedicure. Where the food is nutritious and served three times a day, and family can visit during her stay.

So we searched near and far. Grandma was sick of the car. We wanted the best to put all of our fears at rest.

We finally found a place that was warm and inviting. Not dull or institutional but colourful and exciting. Friendly seniors and staff that answer each residents call.

Singing and dancing and programs with pets. Field trips, fine dining, relaxation and rest.

Six months later

Grandma has since adjusted to long-term care. She has even joined the choir since her placement there. She sits and laughs with her tablemates June, Arthur, and Clive.

Gran goes for exercise classes called "Bodies Alive".

Her well-being is better because of the care.

My friends and I have even started volunteering there.

I am at peace knowing that my Grandma is happy and safe.

She will continue to age with dignity and grace.

www.ingramcontent.com/pod-product-compliance
Lightning Source LLC
LaVergne TN
LVHW072017060526
838200LV00059B/4690